T0354634

Heide R. Kuhlman

Living for the Fruit of the Spirit

◇◇◇◇

Christianity for Those with
Mental Health Conditions

WESTBOW
P R E S S®
A DIVISION OF THOMAS NELSON
& ZONDERVAN

WestBow Press books may be ordered through booksellers or by contacting:

WestBow Press
A Division of Thomas Nelson & Zondervan
1663 Liberty Drive
Bloomington, IN 47403
www.westbowpress.com
844-714-3454

ISBN: 978-1-9736-4195-7 (sc)
ISBN: 978-1-9736-4194-0 (hc)
ISBN: 978-1-9736-4196-4 (e)

Library of Congress Control Number: 2018911987

Print information available on the last page.

WestBow Press rev. date: 07/27/2023

Contents

Chapter One

Why Bother?

When you were born you were given a name. Perhaps you were named after a special someone or for a special reason. You were born into the family of God's choice. You did not choose your eye color, hair color, number of toes, or the blood that is running through your veins. You were born into a specific set of environmental circumstances. You did not choose the number of siblings you have, your position in your family, the family's assets, liabilities, social class, or genetics.

Nor can you change any of these things now. Of course, you can alter some of the things about you that people see. You can change your name, hair color, eye color, or your social class, but you will always have your specific, original details that make you uniquely you—God's creation.

If you are reading this book, it is likely you are a Christian. You believe Jesus died on the cross to save you from your sins. You believe because Jesus died on the cross, your soul will live eternally with God in heaven. This book is designed specifically for Christians. If you are not a believer, my hope and prayer is that you will be open-minded as you read. I pray you will accept Jesus into your heart as your Lord and Savior.

If you are reading this book, you may believe that somehow you got a raw deal in life. Maybe you have a mental health diagnosis, know someone who does, or want to help someone who does. If you are dealing with a mental health condition, then you have had uncomfortable feelings, thoughts, and experiences which have been difficult for you to cope with and understand. Because of your condition and these experiences, you may feel crazy, guilty, afraid, or unloved.

If you are dealing with a mental health condition, there are present and past feelings as well as behaviors and situations that have contributed to your frustration, confusion, and low self-esteem. Perhaps you are sad and disgusted because you have done things you knew better than to do, or you have failed to achieve your personal goals. Perhaps you feel guilty or are frustrated and angry with yourself because you have hurt others or let them down. Perhaps you believe you are not a good Christian and have let God down. In many ways and for many reasons, you may believe you are doomed to be unhappy, dissatisfied, and rejected by the world and all those in it for the rest of your life.

Because you are a Christian, you know that God loves you so much that He sacrificed His Son for you. You know in your head that God has forgiven you for your sins regardless of what they might be. However, because of your mistakes and weaknesses, you may not believe that God likes you very much.

Believe me, I can relate to all these thoughts and many others that are much worse. Keep reading. Try to believe that God will support you in all the necessary ways as you are facing and overcoming those things that continue to haunt you. I will help you understand why you are continuing to have negative thoughts, feelings, and behaviors even though you are doing your very best. I will explain what you need to change in order to realize your potential. I will help you fully understand that God is indeed proud of you and thrilled that you are a part of His family.

Now here comes the "pep talk" which you are probably sick to death of hearing, and there's also a bunch of stuff you might not believe pertains to you. There are things about you that you like and things you do not like. Some of the things you do not like you can change and some things you cannot. God created you the way He did and put you right here, at this time, and in this specific situation for His perfect reasons. God can do no wrong! He does not make mistakes, so you must be perfect in His eyes just the way you are! All the things you do not like and all the challenges you face are put there by God to help you grow and achieve your potential as the best possible Christian you can be. We all want God to help us bypass the pain and the challenges. We feel at times that He has abandoned us, or that His intentions are to punish us in some way. Keep reading! Throughout this book I will point out the rewarding reasons God has led you on your specific faith journey and how your experiences have the potential to enhance your life as a Christian and as a person in general.

If you are finding it challenging to accept what is written in the previous paragraphs, you are not alone. There are all kinds of Christians out there just like you and me who have had the same painful and humiliating experiences that we have had. There are also all kinds of Christians out there who have recovered and continue to grow in their faith journeys, through and despite the challenges they face.

Some people reading this book may have been trying for a lifetime to be good Christians. I could not truly experience God's love for me until after I was forty years old. It took many years, a lot of hard work, and surviving some long, hard struggles before I was ready to receive God's truth about me. I now understand and appreciate many of the reasons God kept me waiting. Every day I look forward to what He continues to reveal to me. I have accepted the fact that everything I have experienced was necessary for me to heal and grow as His child in today's difficult world. I am now grateful for every one of my past experiences, even though many were harsh and painful. God's timing is always perfect! Therefore, I believe the time for you to allow God to reveal Himself to you and to give you some solutions to your challenges is now!

My Testimony

I was brought up to believe that God is good all the time. I was told that I was good because God loved me. But I have not always felt close to God, and I have not always believed that God likes me very much.

I used to think that God gave me a raw deal in life. It seemed to me that I had to deal with a lot more pain and suffering than others did. My faith journey will hopefully help you understand and embrace your own.

My mother and father tried for years to have children. When my mom turned twenty-eight years old in 1957, she was diagnosed with multiple sclerosis (MS). Medical treatments for MS which are common now did not exist then. There was a period when my mother could not even get out of bed.

In 1966, my mother was treated in Rochester, MN with an experimental drug. This medication worked miracles for her! Essentially her MS went into remission. Throughout her life my mother walked with a severe limp and had other mild physical problems, but not so that she could not live a relatively normal and healthy life.

In 1968, my mom got pregnant with me. Not only did she have MS (although in remission) at the time, but she was also forty-one years old. Again, at the time there were not the medical advancements there are now for people with physical disabilities or for people who went through pregnancy and childbirth later in life. Doctors told her I would be abnormal in some way; she was informed that having me would endanger her life. But my mom was stubborn, and she believed that God had enabled her to get pregnant for a reason. She remained strong, and I entered the world in August of 1969.

I may have been a "miracle baby," but I was not born into a healthy family or an easy situation. My father loved me dearly. When I was little, I went everywhere with him, but he battled alcoholism and suffered from severe depression. The older I got, the less my father had to do with me and the less he was available. Knowing what I know now, I believe my mother was bipolar with severe depression. She never let anyone know if her MS bothered her, and she was very smart about hiding her symptoms. But she was also often angry, unreasonable, mean, and very cold. I know now that my parents loved me and were proud of me, but I cannot remember one time when either of them told me so. There were no hugs or comfortable conversations in my family. Life was either quiet and stressful, or loud and explosive. I will never know if my mother yelled and screamed because my father drank and was never around, of if my father drank and was never around because my mother yelled and screamed.

The older I got, the more time I spent anywhere but at home. I learned more and felt more love and acceptance from my friends than from my family. I enjoyed listening to music, reading books, and being at church more than I ever enjoyed being with my parents. I had no siblings, few close family members, and only a few friends, so my childhood was lonely and depressing. Most of the time there was no one to talk to. Because my parents had impossibly high expectations of me, I felt like a failure. Occasionally there were some fun times in our family life, but these were short-lived, and few and far between. There were times at school when I just sat and cried. During the 1970s and 1980s in small-town America, no one wanted to know about your problems or talk to you about theirs. Being sick was never an excuse to miss school in my mom's mind, unless I was throwing up. Experiencing emotional trauma was not even on the radar. Mental health counseling was only for "crazy" people. My father did complete an outpatient drug and alcohol program twice which was good. None of my friends or the other adults in my life, however, ever asked me what was wrong or if I was okay.

Maybe no one noticed, or maybe it was considered nosy to ask about someone else's business.

My parents were Christians, and it was important to them that we maintain the good reputation and the righteous presentation of a perfect family. Every Sunday we sat in the front pew at our Lutheran church. Throughout my school years I spent a lot of time at church and in church activities. I have always believed in God. I have always known that Jesus died for me to be saved. But I did not know God or understand what God's role was in my life. I prayed, sang, studied the Bible, and so on, but I never felt God's presence in me or His direction over my life.

I do not remember an exact moment when I felt God for the first time. It may have been when I was in college choir. We traveled and performed in different churches. One year at Christmas we sang, Handel's *Messiah*, which is a famous, lengthy, and difficult work. There were several times when I felt shivers running down my back during practices and performances. Somehow, I knew when I was singing those words that God was present in the room, in me. Still, I never felt Him interacting with me, and loneliness was my constant companion. I just never seemed to fit anywhere.

As a young adult, I was an overachiever. I got married because everyone else was getting married. I also hoped marriage would alleviate some of the darkness and loneliness in my life. During this season of my life, I went to undergraduate and graduate school. I got involved in different extra-curricular activities. I also worked one or two full-time jobs. All this frenzied activity was while I was busy being pregnant and raising three children. During my late twenties I went through a major move, got divorced, remarried, and built several successful businesses. I hardly ever slept. I was always working on the next big thing. I had the expectation that if or when some situation was resolved or some goal was reached, I would finally be happy. Something or someone would be the key to life being great. I did not realize I was sacrificing my relationships, specifically those with my family and with God, in order to pursue some version of heaven on earth.

Eventually the craziness in my life affected my ability to function. I was catapulting from being unreasonably sad, to overly excited, to intensely angry. I lashed out at the people who loved me and engaged in unhealthy, addictive behaviors. There were times when I had so much energy I did not sleep for days. There were other times when I was so depressed I could not get out of bed. Finally, after my fourth child was born, I was admitted into a mental health hospital and diagnosed with postpartum depression.

The next few years were awful. During this time, I decided to close my private practice of ten years as a licensed mental health counselor. I went through several jobs and made many unhealthy, unreasonable, and unrealistic career and financial decisions. I left home for two days once without contacting my family, sincerely scaring them. I attempted suicide three times. I entered the hospital ten times for various emotional and physical issues. I went from being agitated to depressed to happy to feeling overwhelmed with no rhyme or reason. I didn't know what to expect from myself; my friends and family certainly didn't know what to expect from me.

Eventually I was diagnosed as bipolar with depression and borderline depression. I was also diagnosed with attention deficit disorder. I started getting the right medication and the right mental health counseling. I received electroconvulsive therapy or ECT. I went into the hospital on a monthly basis for treatments. The doctors put me to sleep, attached electrodes to my head, and essentially "rebooted" my brain. I began to feel more stable, and my life improved immensely. With time, as well as with both mental health and spiritual counseling, I have continued to learn from my many mistakes. I am now able to repent and forgive myself and others. I am a work in progress as I move forward on my faith journey in my relationship with God. I am growing in the way I see myself, and in my relationships with others.

For a long time, even though I was receiving the help I needed and things were on the right track, I was still uncomfortable. I felt lost and defeated because it seemed that God had more in store for me and I was not yet living my best life. I felt like the work I was doing on myself and with others was good and contributing to some future mission, but I had no idea what direction to take. I felt empty and discouraged. Once again, I threw myself into different activities and jobs to feel fulfilled in life. I spent time hustling and bustling my children to and from their activities; I volunteered for various things. But I could not escape the feeling that something was out of place or missing. I spent time in prayer and studying God's Word. I had short epiphanies every now and again, but I still felt lost and alone.

Then came a day when God revealed my mission to me. I was driving home from yet another event that had taken me away from my family and my real priorities. I was feeling lost and discouraged. I asked myself aloud in the car, "What do I really want from this life? How do I really want to live, and how do I really want things to be?"

Immediately I heard in my head, "You should be a disciple in my church." I was so shocked I almost drove off the road! God had never communicated with me so directly and so simply before. Looking back now, that was one of the first times I asked God a specific, direct question and then actually listened for His answer! For most of my life I spent a substantial amount of time studying God's Word and being involved in various church activities. But finding fulfillment as a disciple for God or being a leader in my church or my community had never once entered my mind. I never thought of myself as a good enough Christian to serve God in that way. When God revealed to me that my mission in life is to serve Him by reaching out to others, I finally understood how my past and present challenges were going to contribute to my future.

Since then, my relationship with God has continued to evolve in unimaginable ways. I have learned how to communicate with Him; I have learned that His intentions for me are to grow through my experiences during my faith journey. My relationship with God now is more personal, and we communicate through prayer and conversation constantly. I have learned to go to Him when I am feeling angry, afraid, or weak; I have come to trust that He will take care of my troubles. Most importantly, I have learned to listen for God's intentions for me, and sometimes immediately or sometimes with time God will make them known to me. God has become a Father figure to me, and He advises me when I need direction. He is my support system when I am feeling alone, afraid, or anxious. I find peace in God's presence, and it surpasses all understanding. I trust God and seek Him in all ways every day. I understand and appreciate that God created me—flaws and all, each one for a good reason. I accept now that I'm on a need-to-know basis regarding His desires for me and His requirements of me. I know now that God loves me AND likes me. Knowing and appreciating my relationship with God has empowered me to battle my mental health challenges. It has enabled me to forgive myself and those who have wronged me. My relationship with God has provided me with the means to support and help not only myself, but also others through their challenges.

My direction and mission have continued to evolve. My husband and I now own and operate two small Christian retail stores. Because of my faith and the work I have done on my mental health and spiritual issues, I no longer need to attend ECT treatments. I have been blessed in so many incredible and different ways in both my personal and professional lives. I never could have predicted this outcome! I still occasionally have days when life seems to be more difficult than it should be, and I have made mistakes along the way. Yet, I am grateful; I have grown as a Christian through each and every experience that I have weathered even though some were scary and painful.

Enough about me and my story. Let's get back to you. You are likely reading this book because you hope to have more than you have now. You realize that your life has so much more potential. You believe there is something out there that will make your life better. I am here to tell you that you are most certainly right! Keep reading to learn more about the beauty in life that God is ready to reveal to you. He will lead you toward finding the life He wants you to have!

Chapter Two

Who You Are and Who God Is

How many times and in how many ways have you been asked to describe yourself or share your personal information with someone? Don't you hate it when this happens? When someone says to you, "Tell me something about yourself," what are you supposed to say? Sharing casual information is not so bad. I do not mind telling people my name, where I live, who my family members are, and so on. But especially in the beginning of a relationship, I am uncomfortable sharing any details that open me up for judgment.

If you are someone who battles a difficult mental health condition, answering such questions can be challenging. In situations when you are with people you don't know very well, or even sometimes with a gathering of friends, it can be hard to give honest answers to questions like, "How are you doing?" or "What have you been up to?" Generally, it is easiest and best to choose answers that are light and positive. We want to impress others by stating only our best qualities and assets. Others want to hear that life is good for you. Typically, people do not want to burden others with their problems, and they do not want to be burdened by someone else's either. There are times when I want to say, "Do you want me to tell you the truth, or do you want me to tell you what you want to hear?" Sometimes it is easy to think, "Okay—there you are, expecting me to tell you that life is good when I just spent the entire day crying. Or do you really want to hear that I just spent an hour steaming mad because my food was cold when it reached the table?" I am sad to admit that I have lost friends because I thought they cared enough about me to want to know that I was not doing well. I believed I was safe confiding in them because they had confided in me, or I wanted them to confide in me if they did have the need.

There are many reasons those of us who face difficult mental health challenges do not share our true thoughts and feelings. We are afraid to talk about the times we feel depressed for seemingly no viable reason because we do not want to concern others or scare them away. We do not want to admit that we are still upset about something that happened months ago because we embarrassed ourselves or hurt someone. We keep our uncomfortable and negative baggage bottled up inside because we do not want to seem rude or intrusive. Even though we know it would be helpful to talk about what we are going through, we choose not to. It is easier to tell others only what they want to hear. It is more comfortable to share only positive, superficial answers that make people feel good.

It's also an undeniable truth that when we choose to discuss our issues with others, we are forced to face them. We open ourselves up to questions and misunderstandings. This in turn makes it necessary for us to do something about our feelings and whatever issue is at hand. Fixing our problems can be uncomfortable; it requires focus and effort. Doing this seems impossible when you can hardly cope day-to-day. We naturally try to avoid facing pain and heartache whenever our emotional wellbeing requires it.

When living with a difficult mental health condition, it can be challenging to find something positive about yourself. A side-effect of many mental health conditions is that you see yourself uniformly as a useless, sinful, and terrible person. When you have acted in ways that make no sense to yourself or others, you are embarrassed. You are overwhelmed with sadness and anger. Your world is filled with fear because you cannot predict or control your emotions, thoughts, or behaviors, nor can you control how others react to them. You are frustrated because you cannot get anything right. You become depressed when it seems like you are losing the battle to feel good and be productive. You believe you must be stupid because you cannot fix things or because you cannot do things that should come naturally. You become skilled at hiding from your problems and an expert at stuffing them inside.

If you are trying to manage a difficult mental health condition as a Christian, you face additional challenges. When you are overwhelmed, it is easy to believe that God hates you and has abandoned you in your time of need. When you are going through a difficult time, it is hard to believe that there is anything good about a God whom you blame for giving you such an awful life. However, you also feel guilty when you do not treat yourself or others in a Christ-like manner. You know right from wrong, and yet you cannot seem to get it right. The frustration and guilt that comes with failure makes you feel even more guilty, depressed, angry, and scared. You believe that God must hate you, either because He gave you this condition, or because you are not responding to your condition in the expected and correct Christian manner.

When you are battling a mental health condition it can be easy to lose sight of who God created you to be. You cannot see any potential for yourself to be a good Christian. You cannot see yourself living a reasonable, realistic, or healthy life. In fact, when your emotions get too intense, you can become numb and move through your daily life like a zombie. You are out of touch with the world. You simply exist, and nothing more.

It is Not Hopeless!

If you are struggling to understand and appreciate your personality and your unique characteristics, there are formal professional tools available that can help you learn more about who you are. Have you ever taken a test that defines your personality? Some tests ask questions about whether you are outgoing, quiet, creative, or stubborn. I have taken some of these tests and have found some of them to be very helpful. Some measure a person's strengths, or interests and tendencies, or even their weaknesses. I admit that some test results can be disappointing because they can bluntly point out your liabilities and problems for you. But when you use these results to learn about yourself, the tests can help you achieve wisdom and understanding which can help you make healthy decisions.

If you have taken personality assessments, I strongly suggest you have a professional test administrator go over the results with you. I encourage you to ask lots of questions and view the discussion as an opportunity to gain experience with what your strengths are, as well as what you need to work on. If you have not taken assessments and would like to learn more about what your personality tendencies are, you can go online and take some of them yourself. I suggest the Myers Briggs Type Indicator (www. myersbriggs.org) for general personality assessment. A very good assessment is a test called the Kolbe A Index (www.kolbe.com) which measures how people naturally or intuitively act, specifically how they take action, when they are striving. The feedback I have received from the results of these tools has enabled me to manage my depression and stress. Knowing my strengths and weaknesses has helped me tackle them head on and to have awareness of them in challenging situations.

Ecclesiastes 2:26 says, "To the person who pleases him, God gives wisdom, knowledge, and happiness, but to the sinner he gives the task of gathering and storing up wealth to hand it over to the one who pleases God. This too is meaningless, as chasing after the wind." I understand that it can take courage to seek information about yourself when you may not like some of the information you find. But if you do your research and testing with a motivation of seeking wisdom so you may be empowered to treat yourself with kindness, it might be somewhat easier. I do not believe in the saying, "no pain, no gain." You don't necessarily have to suffer in order to grow, even though so many of us do.

But I do believe that with knowledge comes power, and with faith comes courage.

Who Are You in God's Eyes–Really?

When it comes right down to it, does it matter who you perceive yourself to be, or who others perceive you to be? My friend, it does not! Think about it. We live here on earth as God's creations for a very short time! Because of God's grace, we will spend an eternity living as perfect souls in heaven! When you consider things from that perspective, doesn't it make sense to spend the time we have praising, worshipping, and glorifying our Savior, Jesus Christ? After all, it is only by His grace we are saved. Ephesians 2:8-9 states, "God saved you by his *grace when you believed.* And you cannot take credit for this; it is a gift from God. Salvation is not a reward for the good things we have done, so none of us can boast about it" (NLT, italics mine). In other words, believing is the only thing we need to do in order to have salvation and to live eternally in heaven. God clearly says that He already paid for our sins when Jesus died on the cross.

God created you and me. There is no exact definition of who you were created to be. No one is born with a set of instructions. You might think that life would be easier if we were created knowing exactly what our capabilities are and what life has in store for us. God created us in His image; therefore, we have free will and unlimited potential. The book of James in the Bible is one of my favorites. It clearly defines who God wants us to be as Christians in our messed-up world. God presents us with struggles and problems so our faith will be strengthened, and we can develop into mature and responsible Christians. There is no simple or correct way to live your life. Isn't it great that God created us so we can learn from our mistakes instead of being eternally punished by them?

God made each of us to be unique. However, He also created us to have a common mission. As Christians, we know and appreciate that God created us solely for His glory. Have you ever wondered how your existence on earth could possibly benefit God? Perhaps—like me at times—you have known that God loves you but believe that God does not like you very much. Your mental health condition has contributed to the unhealthy and hurtful ways you have managed your emotions, thoughts, and actions. As a result, you feel guilty, irresponsible, and unworthy of God's love.

God did not create us because He needs us to exist. He created us to praise, worship, and glorify Him. We need Him to exist. As Christians, we trust and accept that God always has reasons for what He does. Therefore, we must accept that our existence can glorify God in ways that are pleasing to Him. It seems to me that if our lives were not pleasing to God, He could just wipe us out.

The Bible says that God created us, man and woman, in His own image. Have you ever wondered what this means? To understand the image God created us to be, we first must examine what God's image is.

Because God is so great and powerful, and because he is everywhere at all times, it is difficult to define specifically who God truly is. In the Bible, God is given important, defining characteristics including "love," "peace," "power," and "joy." In several places of the Bible, God defines Himself as the "I am." Sometimes more specific phrases are used to define Jesus, such as, the Light of the World, or the Good Shepherd. The Bible says that He, as our Light and our Shepherd, loves each and every one of us. God does not favor people with specific physical appearances, vibrant characteristics, or emotional compositions. There are, of course, certain actions and behaviors that God prefers.

Those characteristics and behaviors are described as the fruit of the Spirit in Galatians 5:22-23: "But the fruit of the Spirit is love, joy, peace, patience, kindness, goodness, faithfulness, gentleness and self-control; against such things there is no law." More about these later in this book. In general, the Bible does not define which specific personal attributes or abilities each human was created to have. It does not define which specific emotions we were created to feel in different circumstances or on particular occasions. The Bible simply says, "God created mankind in His own image. Male and female, he created them, and he blessed them. God saw all that he had made, and it was very good" (Genesis 1:27-31).

God created us to be different from one another and for our earthly experiences to be unique and productive. God created us to glorify Him, especially when we have such strong faith that we know He will meet all our needs. He created us with the ability to worship and glorify Him as we help others find their needs being met by Him. Furthermore, God provided a divine and supernatural means for us to worship and glorify Him through the power of the Holy Spirit in this lifetime while we are on this earth.

Chapter Three

Knowing and Experiencing God

So now you are asking yourself, "Communication with God? Who does that? Is that even possible?" I assure you, it is possible, and it does not really take a ton of effort either. Here are some suggestions for you when you desire to have a personal and healthy conversation with God.

"[God] says, 'Be still, and know that I am God; I will be exalted among the nations, I will be exalted in the earth'" (Psalm 46:10). For me, the most difficult part of prayer and meditation is contained in this verse. With all of life's distractions it can be difficult to simply "be still and know," but this is a necessary part of getting in touch with God. The first time I ever heard God's voice was when I was driving in my car, and I asked God a specific question. Then I listened intently for the answer. Prayer is important and special. It requires focus, peace, and stillness. I know that sometimes when we pray or say the Lord's Prayer, we do so without taking the time to really think about and feel the words. If you desire to have God's attention and desire for Him to listen to your prayers, thoughts, and feelings then you must do the same for Him.

For those of us with mental health issues this can be especially difficult. Our minds are busy with overwhelming and depressing thoughts while we process difficult issues. I have an attention deficit disorder diagnosis, so I know I must be especially careful when I pray. I need to put my mind into neutral and truly focus on God and upon honoring Him with respect and care. If you struggle in this area you can practice by reading the Bible, then thinking and writing about what you are reading. A good study Bible can be especially helpful. I recommend the *Life Application Study Bible* by Tyndale House Publishers if you are in the market for one which will help you apply the Bible to your life. It comes in several translations, and there are versions appropriate for childhood through various stages of adult life. There are also many Christian devotionals which can help you stay focused on God. The devotional, *Jesus Calling* by Sarah Young, is one of my favorites. It is written in the first person, so reading it is like having God speak to you directly. Journaling your thoughts and feelings about what you are reading in the Bible or a devotional is also important. This can help you fully ingest what you are reading. More about that later.

I have found it essential to have a clear picture of God's presence during prayer. Before I start my prayers, I like to close my eyes and picture what Jesus' presence in my life looks, smells, sounds, feels, and tastes like. Because I am in love with the ocean, I like to imagine Jesus with me walking along the shore. When I do this, I feel especially close to God, and I find it easy to understand that He is right there with me. When I concentrate, I can see Jesus and smell the ocean air. I can perceive what it feels like; I can imagine the sounds and even the tastes in that place at that moment.

For you, the picture may be different, but because God is present everywhere and in every way, it should not be too much of a stretch to find a niche where you can imagine yourself alone with God. Perhaps you are simply sitting with God on a park bench, or maybe you can envision Him sitting on the edge of your bed. When you take time to go through each of the five senses during your time with God, it can be rewarding and easy to imagine God is right there with you. Remember, God sees it as an honor when you focus on Him. You are demonstrating respect when you put purpose and effort into your time with Him. The experience can be rewarding for you both.

Next, start your verbal and non-verbal communication with God. A simple way to do this is to write a letter to God. Begin by expressing your love and appreciation for Him; then ask some honest and sincere questions. Because God knows what you are going to ask before you do, you cannot get it wrong. Your communication should be personal and again, honest. Feel free to unload your anger and resentment as well as your depression and grief. God gets it. He understands and appreciates what you are going through.

Finally, let the process work for you. I like to continue by writing a letter from God back to me. Those thoughts and feelings that are flowing are God's special words, thoughts, and feelings just for you! Be prepared for anything because God's words may be a bit shocking, or perhaps they will feel familiar to you. I suggest that you write down whatever you hear so you can process it later. If you hear the thoughts coming rapidly, try your best to keep up. Do not worry though, because God never gives you more that you can handle without His guidance to see you through. If the thoughts and feelings come slowly, that is okay too. It just means that your God is taking His time to explain things to you. He'll give you bite-size thoughts of His message to you, and He'll do it in a way that you understand and appreciate. He might speak of uncomfortable things—things you do not want to hear, such as "wait and see," or "not now." But you can feel safe knowing that God heard you and He cares enough to share with you what you now know. Perhaps He will suggest a means of coping for you. He will reassure you that you can trust His judgment. At any rate, anything that comes from God is a blessing!

If writing is not your thing-and that is all right—but please try it before you consider not doing it. Writing slows the process down so you can be sure you receive the messages correctly. Once you are comfortable hearing God's voice, the sometimes-rapid-fire but usually constant conversation between you and God will establish itself. I especially like writing everything down because it creates a record for me to process and reread later. I can easily remind myself of where I was and how far I have come.

Establishing an ongoing, working relationship with God has been especially rewarding and helpful for me. Experiencing God's presence first-hand in my life has enabled me to find, establish, and maintain good health habits and stability in spite of my mental health issues. The loneliness I have often felt for so many years has essentially disappeared. I now feel confident and at peace knowing that I can go to God with anything and everything, and He will be present in my prayers.

Now, more about God's personality and the things that make Him tick. Yes, you heard me correctly. It honestly is not difficult to understand God or to see where He is coming from. His intentions for you are within your grasp. Put simply, the answers lie within Scripture and the fruit of the Spirit.

Chapter Four

What Use You Can Be to God

Jesus' personality was intimately described in the Bible. The Word of God, of course, implies that Jesus was both God and man, and He is perfect in every way. Still, it is interesting to me that at no time does the Bible describe Jesus as having any personality traits which are unattainable for us. While on earth, Jesus repeatedly demonstrated the characteristics of the fruit of the Spirit—love, joy, peace, patience, kindness, goodness, faithfulness, gentleness, and self-control. We are capable of having and displaying each one of these wonderful characteristics. They are not unattainable. We can be like Jesus.

There is a good reason the Bible shares many of God's most intimate qualities. The descriptions are not only there so we can fully comprehend who God is. They are there so we can understand who we are with respect to God. They are there so we can appreciate who God created each of us to be. Being created in God's image does not mean that we were created to be exactly like God. It means that we were created to give glory to God's existence, enabling Him to be glorified through our thoughts, words, and actions.

There are many terms used in the Bible to describe God. These can also be found in Bible dictionaries, commentaries, and concordances. I will list a few here because I believe it is very important for us to understand exactly who God is and how we relate to Him and through Him to the world around us.

First, God is our Creator. He created us and all of His creation where we live. He created us to care for His world, for ourselves, for others, and for all living things. We are to nurture and care for God's creation in all the ways that are reasonable, realistic, and healthy during our lifetimes. God also created us to honor Him by giving thanks and praise for all that exists. Ultimately, we are also to promote God's mission by encouraging and engaging others to care for His world.

God declared in Exodus 3:14 that we should call Him the "I Am," which infers that God is the only one who has always and will always exist. Again, this infers that we exist to give thanks and praise to God for creating us, and we are to promote God's mission by encouraging and engaging others to follow God's Word.

Another term used in the Bible to describe God is Adonai, which means "Lord" or "Master." God alone exists as our ruler and the Master of all living things. Because this is true, we are to obey Him just as it is written in the Bible. We are to live eagerly and excitedly as we serve Him, which in turn expresses honor and appreciation for all He has done.

God is commonly known as our provider. He has always and will forever provide all that is necessary for life to exist. All we need to do is have faith and accept God's gifts. We thank God, praise Him, and promote His mission by encouraging and engaging others to do the same.

As our shepherd, God guides and protects us. All we need is faith that God's plans for us are good. We simply need patience and appreciation for His will even when we are not able to understand His directions for us at the time.

My favorite term used to describe God is love. God's love for us is so incredible that there are not words to describe it. Love is the reason God never abandons us even when we reject Him. He loves us dearly, constantly, and consistently in every way no matter what our thoughts, words, or deeds are. All God expects from us is to love Him and others by having faith in Him, listening to Him, and trusting Him every day in every way.

Finally, God most definitely is peace. He enables us to live in His peace through His love when we trust and have faith that He will meet our needs. God rewards us by enabling us to have peace in our lives here on earth. He makes His presence known to us whenever we experience peace through Him. All we are expected to do is to give thanks and praise to God for loving us and meeting our needs. Then we can experience peace and share that peace with others.

Just what does God want from me?

> So I say, live by the Spirit, and you will not gratify
> the desires of the flesh. (Gal. 5:16)

> The acts of the flesh are obvious: sexual
> immorality, impurity and debauchery; idolatry
> and witchcraft; hatred, discord, jealousy, fits of
> rage, selfish ambition, dissensions, factions and
> envy; drunkenness, orgies, and the like, I warn
> you, as I did before, that those who live like
> this will not inherit the kingdom of God." (Gal.
> 5:19-21)

> Since we live by the Spirit, let us keep step with
> the Spirit. Let us not become conceited, provoking
> and envying each other. (Gal. 5:25-26)

> For the sinful nature desires what is contrary to
> the Spirit, and the Spirit what is contrary to the
> sinful nature. They are in conflict with each other,
> so that you do not do what you want. (Gal. 5:17)

The Bible indeed clarifies what God expects from us. He
expects us to will follow His commandments, adhere to His
Word, and not give in to that little voice inside that says, "Yes! Yes!
Yes!" to sin when the response should be "No! No! No!"

The above verses state readily what God does not want from
us, especially Galatians 5:19-21. So, what does God want and

expect from us? What does it mean to realize your potential as a Christian in a fallen world? The book of Galatians contains one clear answer to these questions.

> But the fruit of the Spirit is love, joy, peace, forbearance, kindness, goodness, faithfulness, gentleness and self-control. Against such things there is no law. Those who belong to Christ Jesus have crucified the flesh with its passions and desires. Since we live by the Spirit, let us keep in step with the Spirit. Let us not become conceited, provoking and envying each other. (Gal. 5:22-23)

In the following chapters I will discuss each trait of the fruit of the Spirit. I will show how living a life that exemplifies these qualities enables you to realize your potential as a Christian and to live a strong, healthy, positive life.

Chapter Five

Realizing Your Fullest Potential

Let us summarize what we have discussed so far. We have examined and defined who we are as children of God. We have identified God's expectations for us. We have discussed who God is and what His role is in our lives. We have established how God relates to us when we are challenged with ongoing difficult situations. We have assessed the reasons God chose you to face your specific challenges at this time.

Armed with this information, we are ready to face the elephant in the room: it's time for us to discuss how to live a reasonable, realistic, and healthy lifestyle as a Christian with mental health issues.

What are reasonable and realistic expectations for a Christian who is challenged by mental health issues?

This may seem like an impossible and unfair question. The reason this question is difficult is because it has no single perfect answer. The better question may be, "How will I know if or when

I am realizing my potential in a reasonable and realistic Christian life?"

We have already discussed what it is like when you are experiencing the opposite of a healthy Christian lifestyle. If you have a mental health condition you may not even know what it is like to experience life as a reasonable, realistic, or healthy individual.

In the book of Deuteronomy, God spoke to His people through Moses. These verses describe how life would be for the Israelites if they chose not to love or follow God.

> You will live in constant suspense, filled with dread both night and day, never sure of your life. In the morning you will say, "If only it were evening!" and in the evening, "If only it were morning!"—because of the terror that will fill your hearts and the sights that your eyes will see. (Deut. 28:66-67)

These verses accurately describe the way I used to be when I was not doing well. More direct words that explain what I experienced include: anxious, depressed, angry, overwhelmed, and ultimately, scared. If I had to choose one or two words to describe myself and my life during those challenging times, they would be "empty" and "chaotic." Therefore, I am summarizing an "unreasonable, unrealistic, and unhealthy" lifestyle as "empty and chaotic."

The Gifts of the Holy Spirit

> Peter replied, "Repent and be baptized, every
> one of you, in the name of Jesus Christ for the
> forgiveness of your sins. And you will receive the
> gift of the Holy Spirit." (Acts 2:38)

For those who are new believers or are unfamiliar with the
work of the Holy Spirit, here is a very brief introduction to how
He came to be in our lives and of how He works. After Jesus was
raised from the dead on the third day He met with his disciples
for forty days. During this important interval, Jesus taught the
disciples more about what they needed to know to go out into
the world and share the good news. Just before Jesus ascended
into heaven, He told the disciples to wait for the Holy Spirit to
supernaturally and divinely descend from heaven. When the Holy
Spirit did descend from heaven, He entered into the disciples and
empowered them with the gift of the Holy Spirit. All believers
carry this with them in various forms to this day.

Below are verses that thoroughly define the gifts of the Holy
Spirit. Throughout the Bible there are countless references to these
gifts; they are not to be confused with the fruit of the Spirit. There
have been countless books and studies done on the aspects of the
gifts of the Spirit as well. I encourage you to study and research
them more. That effort will help you proceed with self-discovery
in determining which of these gifts God has blessed you with; you
will be called to use them to fulfill your greatest potential during
the short time you are on this earth. The verses below explain what

happened soon after Jesus ascended into heaven after the forty days He spent on the earth following His resurrection.

> Now to each one the manifestation of the Spirit is given for the common good. To one there is given through the Spirit a message of wisdom, to another a message of knowledge by means of the same Spirit, to another faith by that one Spirit, to another miraculous powers, to another prophecy, to another distinguishing between spirits, to another speaking in different kinds of tongues, and to still another the interpretation of tongues. All these are the work of one and the same Spirit, and he distributes them to each one, just as he determines. (1 Cor. 12: 7-11)

I understand that for a new believer or a hesitant one, some of these might sound somewhat farfetched. It can be difficult to understand and appreciate that the Father, the Son, and the Holy Spirit are indeed one Holy God. With regards to the Holy Spirit, the entire Bible consists of descriptions of the role the Holy Spirit has played throughout history. From miracles to healings to even a message in the form of a burning bush, the Holy Spirit has been a loyal and active member of the Trinity; He will continue to work in all of us for eternity.

When I consider the gifts of the Spirit and that God willingly bestows these supernatural phenomena among all His believers, I am in awe! It simply humbles me as a child of God to know that He trusts me with such a sacred gift and to have an ability from Him. To think that God never gives us more than we can handle and provides for our every need every minute of every day!

Regarding the gifts of the Holy Spirit and as someone dealing with a mental health condition, know this: the gifts of the Holy Spirit are present in you to help you through any and every challenge you face. God is there to empower you in whatever way you need. He will give you the ability to face and handle any challenges that may come your way! It might not always feel like it. It might not always seem like it. You may struggle along the way to believe God is present in your life. You may question the reasons He is challenging you in the ways that He is. My friend, God is all-powerful, always present, and able to handle anything. All you need to do is take your problems to Him. His shoulders are indeed big enough!

These are my favorite Bible verses for this topic:

I can do all this through him who gives me strength. (Phil. 4:13)

Trust in the Lord with all your heart and lean not on your own understanding. In all your ways submit to him, and he will make your paths straight. (Prov. 3:5-6)

Are you asking yourself what you need to do now to receive the gifts of the Spirit and how to achieve stability and saneness as a Christian? My friend, the answer to this question is to simply to ask! It's as easy as 1-2-3!

1. 1Pray for the power of the Holy Spirit.
2. Wait for God's strength to carry you through.
3. Trust and have faith that what goes up, will come down!

Prayer and the Holy Spirit

There is certainly a common denominator for all the things God wants us to do in life, and that is constant and consistent prayer! What goes up, must come down. Prayer is the way we invite God to intervene in our lives. It is the way we show God how much we love and appreciate Him. It is the way we worship, praise, and glorify Him. If you are struggling at all in your life, you are not spending enough time or the right kind of time in prayer!

One of my favorite books is *The 21 Most Effective Prayers in the Bible* by James Earley. The author lists a few things prayer accomplishes:

- Prayer is the way you defeat the devil. (Luke 22:23; James 4:7)
- Prayer is the way you get the lost saved. (Luke 18:13)
- Prayer is the way you acquire wisdom. (James 1:5)
- Prayer is the way a backslider gets restored. (James 5:16-20)
- Prayer is how saints get strengthened. (Jude 20; Matt. 26:41)

- Prayer is the way to get laborers out to the mission field. (Matt. 9:38)
- Prayer is how we cure the sick. (James 5:13-15)
- Prayer is how we accomplish the impossible. (Mark 11:23-24)

In the following verses, the disciples ask Jesus how they should pray. Jesus teaches the disciples to pray the Lord's Prayer.

> One day Jesus was praying in a certain place. When he finished, one of his disciples said to him, "Lord, teach us to pray just as John [the Baptist] taught the disciples." He said to them, "When you pray, say: 'Father, hallowed be your name, your kingdom come. Give us each day our daily bread. Forgive us our sins, for we also forgive everyone who sins against us. And lead us not into temptation.'" (Luke 11:1-4)

Friend, one of the greatest things about prayer is that there is no single correct way to pray. I pray continuously throughout the day. My favorite time is while I am driving to work in the mornings or home in the evenings. I give thanks and praise for my family members and all the wonderful things God has done for me in my life. I ask for help, guidance, and courage to face difficult challenges as they come up. I ask for peace and comfort when I am in pain. Again, prayer can come in many different forms. I spend time worshipping and glorifying God when I sing and play the piano. The most important thing to remember about prayer is to just do it. God wants to be a part of your life! Invite Him in through prayer.

> "Ask, and it will be given to you; seek, and you will find; knock and the door will be opened to you. For everyone who asks receives; the one who seeks finds; and to the one who knocks, the door will be opened." (Matt. 7:7-8)

> Therefore confess your sins to each other and pray for each other so that you may be healed. The prayer of a righteous person is powerful and effective. (James 5:16)

God's Just Rewards for You!

What can you expect your life to be like when you allow the Holy Spirit in and allow God to take control? How can you expect God to respond when you worship, give thanks, and praise Him for all he has done for you? The answer is so simple. In short, what goes around, comes around. The verses that describe the fruit of the Spirit in Galatians are some of my most treasured verses. They define God's response to me when I respond to people and my environment in healthy, realistic, and reasonable ways. I know when I treat people and situations in my life with love, joy, peace, patience, kindness, goodness, faithfulness, gentleness, and self-control that I can expect God to treat me with these qualities also.

I spend my life craving and thriving on these beautiful rewards from God—the fruit of the Spirit!

Did you know your emotions travel eighty thousand times faster than your thoughts? It is hard enough for a "normal" person to manage intense feelings in healthy ways. It is exceptionally hard for those of us with challenging mental health conditions to do so. Our brains play tricks on us. The unhealthy seem intense and unbearable. Therefore, uncomfortable things appear to be life-threatening. When things appear to be life-threatening, we are tempted to think and act in ways that benefit Satan instead of God or ourselves. Sometimes we even know that the things we do are wrong beforehand or as we are doing them. We act inappropriately anyway because the emotion that drives the wrong behavior is so intense we feel we have no choice but to charge forward.

When we take the time to slow down, close our eyes, breathe, pray, and give the problem to God, He will empower us to rise to any occasion and proceed through anything! We may not feel empowered immediately. It may take quite a lot of time and much continuous prayer. It can be hard work to let go of the control over our own situations, especially when emotions are intense or you have reached panic mode. It may require practice and diligence to establish the habit of giving all your problems to God. But friend, the rewards are great and the effort is worthwhile! When you have reached the other side of that challenge, the love and peace you feel are even more intense than the messed-up thoughts and feelings you left behind. Trust me, it is so worth it.

I understand why you might still be hesitant to trust that this will work. For starters, God's work is not always something that can be seen. He often works behind the scenes and His timing might seem slow as He make things right. Also, there are some situations or problems that cannot be reversed—a death for example. Friend, God uses each and every situation for the benefit of all in some way and in His time. You may not recognize His handiwork right away. It might help to spend some time in God's presence, asking Him to show you how things come to light for His glory.

When things are not going well for you, I challenge you to be open-minded and grateful that things are not worse. It's honoring to God when you recognize your blessings even if it looks like the bad outweighs the good. Pick up your Bible. Read it. Search for solace in the Psalms, look for wisdom in Proverbs, and seek answers in the Gospels and the letters of the New Testament. Every time I dive into God's Word, I discover something about myself that makes me grateful for all I have, and I constantly crave to learn more! I have been on the edge of suicide many times during my life. I have even allowed myself to go over the edge more than once. Each time I have reached bottom it has always been by God's wonderful grace that I have pulled through. I have come through a better Christian and a better person. I am more equipped and empowered to glorify and serve God in ways I never thought possible.

I love how God designed the fruit of the Spirit for us! Did you notice that the word "fruit" is singular? This is unlike the "gifts" of the Holy Spirit, with which God rewards believers a minimum of one or perhaps more gifts. In Galatians, it says we are entitled to each aspect of a singular fruit. God's promise to us all is that we are each entitled to love, joy, peace, patience, kindness, goodness, gentleness, faithfulness, and self-control infinitely and completely. All we need to do is pray and ask. What a grand God we have!

In the next few chapters I will share how each aspect of the fruit of the Spirit can bring happiness and stability, especially to those with mental health conditions. I will break down each aspect of the fruit of the Spirit into three ways in which the Spirit shines through us. I will demonstrate how the fruit is revealed in our relationships with God, our relationships with others, and our perceptions of ourselves.

I understand you may be skeptical. I understand you may believe you have tried it all. I appreciate that you may believe you are destined to live your life in misery. You may even be questioning how a solution with no scientific data can possibly work for you. Friend, I have been there so many times. So if you have tried it all, what is it to try one more thing? What have you really got to lose? You are reading this book, so you may as well give it a go. I'm praying for you and cheering you on! And so is God, every minute and every step of the way!

Chapter Six

The Love of the Holy Spirit

It always protects, always trusts, always hopes, always perseveres. Love never fails. (1 Cor. 13:7-8)

This is how we know what love is: Jesus Christ laid down his life for us. And we ought to lay down our lives for our brothers and sisters. Dear children, let us not love with words or speech but with actions and in truth. (1 John 3:16,18)

Love For and From God

The one word we can always use to describe God is "love." There are many words used to explain love because it is a complicated concept, but no words can accurately describe the love that God has for us. We all know that God loves us so much that He sacrificed His perfect Son to pay for our sins, thus providing for our salvation. We can see God's love for us in all of His creation. We can feel God's love for us when we repent for our mistakes.

It's a mystery how God can continue to love us as He does as we consider the mess we have made of His world. It is no wonder we have so many problems when we have removed God from our schools, we shoot each other in the streets, and we have chosen to seek personal vendettas against those who sin against us. Instead, we should be giving God the opportunity to be the judge He rightfully is.

There is definitely a reason the word "love" appears in the Bible 646 times. If the entire Bible was summed up in one verse, it would be John 3:16: "For God so loved the world that he gave is only begotten Son that whosoever believes in him will have eternal life."

The verses below provide a biblical definition of what love truly is.

> Love is patient, love is kind. It does not envy, it does not boast, it is not proud. It does not dishonor others, it is not self-seeking, it is not easily angered, it keeps no record of wrongs. Love does not delight in evil but rejoices with the truth. It always protects, always trusts, always hopes, always perseveres. Love never fails. And now these three remain: faith, hope and love. But the greatest of these is love. (1 Cor. 13:4-8,13)

For most of us, God's love is not a secret or an unfamiliar subject. However, we do not always take the time to consider how much and in what ways God loves us. From the beginning—literally—God has loved us. God loved Adam and Eve even though they committed the first sin. God loves us so much that He sacrificed His own Son, and thus made it possible for our souls to have eternal life with Him in heaven. God loves us when we honor Him with our prayers and praises. God also loves us when we ignore Him, disrespect Him, and hurt each other. God does not pick and choose. God loves all of us, all of the time!

Stop and think for a moment exactly what that means for you and for God. Try to put yourself in God's place. Would you stick around after your children abandoned you, hurt you, and horrified you? Would you decide that this world is not worth the time or the trouble? Would you be able to fully forgive and offer the gift of eternal life, even to those who create chaos in this world? God considers all believers to be His children. He loves us even more than you love your own children knowing their faults. God loves us unconditionally and with a power and an intensity that no words can describe.

Considering this, how can we begin to show love to God, sinners that we are? Because God is so great and because God is who He is, He deserves a love that is greater than we can give! That's okay. God does not expect perfection from us because He knows that we are not perfect. He appreciates the hardships we go through. We can grow and our faith gets stronger when we enable Him to be a partner with us in our challenges. God only expects us to do the best we can.

To be healthy you need to use every available opportunity to show God how much you love Him. Make it your mission, as I have, to thank God, to praise Him, and to glorify Him every day of your life. Do your very best to follow God's Word, pray often and intently, and give God control of every aspect of your life. What goes up will indeed come down, and in turn, you will receive God's love and be blessed with God's guidance and presence in your life!

Love For and From Others

Above all, love each other deeply, because love covers over a multitude of sins. (1 Peter 4:8)

Finally, all of you, live in harmony with one another; be sympathetic, love as brothers, be compassionate and humble. (1 Peter 3:8)

A new commandment I give you: Love one another. As I have loved you, so you must love one another. By this all men will know that you are my disciples, if you love one other. (John 13:34-35)

"Teacher, which is the greatest commandment in the Law?" Jesus replied, "'Love the Lord your God with all your heart and with all your soul and with all your mind.' This is the first and greatest commandment. And the second is like it: 'Love your neighbor as yourself.' All the Law and the Prophets hang on to these two commandments." (Matt. 22:36-40)

That is it. It is that simple. Except that it is not. The first part of God's greatest commandment—loving God—can be harder than loving your neighbor. God's presence is not always evident in our thoughts, and therefore it is easy to take His glory for granted. But regardless of our mistakes and faults, God always loves us back.

The second part of the greatest commandment can be more challenging. It refers to loving your neighbor. In this case your neighbor refers to anyone and everyone who is not you. Did you just sigh deeply at this one? I get it! Many of us have a history with all those others that is difficult. Loving some people despite their faults is not easy. In cases of abuse and neglect or other equally horrific situations, it may even seem unjust, impossible, or just plain wrong.

One way to love your neighbor is to forgive them. Did you just sigh deeply again at this suggestion? Does forgiving your neighbor seem impossible right now? Bear with me! Forgiving your neighbor does not mean you should forget the past or what you have been through. Forgiving others is something you do for you, not the person who has harmed you or others. It's something you do because God commanded it in Colossians 3:13. "Bear with each other and forgive one another if any of you has a grievance against someone. Forgive as the Lord forgave you." It also says in Luke 17:4, "Even if they sin against you seven times in a day and seven times come back to you saying, 'I repent', you must forgive them." Finally, in Ephesians 4:32 the Word says, "Be kind and compassionate to one another, forgiving each other, just as in Christ God forgave you." Forgiveness is something you do because it is the right thing to do. Remember, God has forgiven you, and He continues to forgive you of your sins— all of them. If He can do it, you can do it with His guidance and help.

Another way we show love to our neighbors is by not judging them. I know this may again seem to be an impossible goal. All of us judge others sometimes, whether it is intentional or not. When we describe other people, we relate their physical attributes and personality traits—the heavy-set lady, or the boy who has an impressive jump shot, the ethnic-specific man, and so on. We probably assume things about people based on those attributes and traits and our judgment of them.

The Bible says in Luke 6:37, "Do not judge, and you will not be judged. Do not condemn, and you will not be condemned. Forgive, and you will be forgiven." Ask yourself often whether you are passing judgment on others. Consider your thoughts, feelings, and behaviors as if God is watching you and all of your actions and reactions because He actually is. Are you able to be proud in what you see? Do you believe you are doing your absolute best to follow God's Word for His expectations of a good Christian? If you are, then you are living with love. You are living with respect to the fruit of the Holy Spirit and God will indeed reward you with His love in return.

I understand it is hard to forgive, to be compassionate, and to not judge. Remember, God is with you. Continually pray and ask God to help you and guide you. Be patient and wait for Him to help you manage your emotions, thoughts, and actions. James 1:12 says, "Blessed is the one who perseveres under trial because, having stood the test, that person will receive the crown of life that the Lord has promised to those who love him."

Love For Yourself

I admit that loving myself is one of the most difficult challenges I face. I find it easy to find fault with myself. I can be oversensitive to the criticism of others. I feel guilty when I inadvertently hurt anyone or do any kind of damage in this world. I want to believe I am essentially good. However, I also have those days when it is hard to recognize something good that I have going for me. I often find it hard to receive love from others. I have a tough time believing that I deserve love from someone else because of things I have done or said in my past, or because I am having a difficult time now managing my symptoms in a reasonable, realistic, or healthy way.

There are not a lot of verses in the Bible that refer to self-esteem. Even so, it is obvious that God finds it necessary for us to love ourselves, believe in ourselves, and take care of ourselves. God's greatest commandment, to love our neighbors as ourselves is mentioned in the Bible at least eight times. Let's break this commandment down.

You are commanded to love your neighbor. You are also commanded to love yourself. You are not commanded to love your neighbor any more than you love yourself. And let me stress that you are indeed commanded to love yourself, flaws and all!

So, what does it mean to love yourself? It certainly does not mean that you should go about flaunting your gifts. First Peter

5:6 says, "Humble yourselves, therefore, under God's mighty hand, that he may lift you up in due time." You should adhere to God's greatest commandment to the best of your ability. Your compliant nature will then have love, joy, peace, patience, kindness, goodness, gentleness, faithfulness, and self-control.

When I consider how I can best fulfill my potential as a good Christian, the Serenity Prayer says it all:

> God, give me the serenity to accept the things
> cannot change, the wisdom to change the things I
> can, and the courage to know the difference.

That is all, that is it. It is that simple. Except, again, that it is not. When your emotions become overwhelming and your thoughts are on fire, it is not so easy. That is why we go to God in our times of need! It is why we need to engage in constant and continuous prayer for God's help and guidance. Our reward for doing so is great! Psalm 25:9 says, "He guides the humble in what is right and teaches them his way." Let God show you His way, and when you live by the fruit of the Holy Spirit, you will be rewarded with love beyond your wildest expectations or imagination.

> This is how we know that we belong to the truth
> and how we set our hearts at rest in his presence:
> If our hearts condemn us, we know that God is
> greater than our hearts, and he knows everything.
> Dear friends, if our hearts do not condemn us,
> we have confidence before God and receive
> from Him anything we ask, because we keep

his commands and do what pleases him. And this is his command: to believe in the name of his Son, Jesus Christ, and to love one another as he commanded us. The one who keeps God's commands lives in him, and he in them. And this is how we know that he lives in us: We know it by the Spirit he gave us." (1 John 3:19-24)

Chapter Seven

The Joy of the Holy Spirit

At that time Jesus, full of joy through the Holy Spirit, said, "I praise you, Father, Lord of heaven and earth, because you have hidden these things from the wise and learned, and revealed them to the little children. Yes, Father, for this is what you were pleased to do." (Luke 10:21)

"If you keep my commands, you will remain in my love, just as I have kept my Father's commands and remain in his love. I have told you this so that my joy may be in you and that your joy may be complete." (John 15:10-11)

Those the Lord has rescued will return. They will enter Zion with singing; everlasting joy will crown their heads. Gladness and joy will overtake them, and sorrow and sighing will flee away. (Isa. 51:11)

Joy For and From God

Joy is the result of knowing that Jesus has secured our eternal lives through salvation on the cross. It is also the result of celebrating and reveling in God's creation, living our lives as God intended, and by our efforts to relate in God's way to God's people. The word "joy" is mentioned four hundred and thirty times in the Bible; it is obviously special.

When we discover Jesus and the supernatural effect of His influence on us and on His creation, we are rewarded with joy. It is the miracle of life!

One only must be present at a sunrise or watch a video on YouTube about cute kittens or sneezing baby pandas to find reasons to rejoice in God's creation. Joy comes naturally and simply through God. Sadly, for those dealing with mental health issues, these kinds of joys tend to be surface joys. They are easily taken for granted and are quickly replaced with ugliness and misery as we struggle to keep our misery concealed. If you ask anyone who struggles with a mental health condition about the joy they experience regularly in their lives, they will likely find it hard to identify constant or consistent sources and occasions.

It is easy to have joy in God's grace when you consider what we have been saved from. We are a fallen population in a fallen society. God's influence in this world when we allow Him to work through us is no small feat. The influences in our culture tend to cloud God's grace and glory unless we remind ourselves of God's existence every day. It's common to develop what I call a "yeah, but" syndrome for things that go wrong for us. Instead of simply rejoicing because God has saved us from our sins by grace through faith, we say, "Yeah, God is great, but…." We allow ourselves to be overcome with anxiety, anger, and depression. We function constantly as overwhelmed people in a fast-paced society that undervalues the reasons and relationships that can result in joy for us. The world God created for us, especially if we consider only our need for survival, is so incredibly simple. Yet we choose to allow things that complicate our lives to receive most of our attention. When we simply focus our attention on God, on His Word, and on His intentions, we can experience incessant and overwhelming joy.

Joy for Self and for Others

The only genuine joy is in God. It is not in things or in circumstances. Some of my most self-defeating and disappointing moments have been when I lost sight of God's involvement in my life. Instead, I chose to believe I would only be happy when this, that, or the other thing happened.

God reveals Himself to us through the good, the bad, and the ugly. Believe it or not, one way we receive joy from God even as we struggle through the difficult times is through His interactions with us as well as His restoration of us. When we proceed through the challenges of this world, joy accompanies our sense of accomplishment. When we abide in God and in His Word then we can let go to allow God control. If we trust Him to provide for us, we are rewarded with joy. Often through prayer, I am reminded that God will provide for my every need.

When I refer all my cares and concerns to Him, it always picks me up because I have faith that God will provide the best for me in His time.

It is hard to believe for those with mental health conditions that through God we all receive joy. Having some relief from symptoms by simply enjoying God seems to be too simple; it is easier to believe that God does not care or does not exist. Many with mental health conditions come from abusive environments and relationships which is an added complication. And many doctors and counselors are problem- and symptom-focused rather than being God- and solution-focused. Finally, because many with mental health conditions struggle to manage their symptoms, they are reluctant to let God take care of them. They are afraid if they let go of the little control they believe they now have, they will lose it completely. Sadly, the opposite is true.

Those with mental health conditions who find ways to appreciate God and enable Him to work supernaturally in their lives are being courageous. God generously rewards these souls by enabling them to achieve a higher level of function which naturally results in precious joy!

God rewards those who forgive people who have wronged them with joy and peace! For those with mental health conditions, forgiveness of self and others can be complicated and difficult. Those who can give God control of all the things they cannot control, find joy through God! Satan loves those who hang onto bitterness and guilt. He wreaks havoc in their lives, possessing them and leading them to experience anxiety and anger. To let go and give God control may not be the easiest thing to do, but it is possible when a conscious effort is made to do so. Those who practice prayer and meditation as well as take care to remain calm when cultural influences and life circumstances are hammering away at them are rewarded with joy and peace.

In the end, you can decide to be problem-focused or God-focused. You can choose grudges, or you can have joy. I know which ones I am choosing. How about you?

Chapter Eight

The Peace of the Holy Spirit

But now in Christ Jesus you who once were far away have been brought near through the blood of Christ. For He Himself is our peace. (Eph. 2:13-14)

"Peace I leave with you; my peace I give you. I do not give to you as the world gives. Do not let your hearts be troubled and do not be afraid." (John 14:27)

The kingdom of God is not a matter of eating and drinking, but of righteousness, peace and joy in the Holy Spirit. (Rom. 14:17)

The mind of sinful man is death, but the mind controlled by the Spirit is life and peace. (Rom. 8:6)

Peace From God

When I think of the peace that comes from God, my role model is Jesus. Now there is a man who did not falter despite horrendous environmental and physical circumstances. He resisted temptation when Satan led Him into the wilderness. He worked miracles in people like Thomas and Saul—who became Paul—when they doubted Him.

When Jesus died on the cross He literally carried the sins of the world on His back. The Bible says that in the garden of Gethsemane Jesus prayed so fervently that He sweated blood. And yet in the end, Jesus experienced divine peace as He died on the cross. His final words, "It is finished," resonate in my heart. Jesus came to earth as both man and God and proved that even in the most brutal of circumstances it is possible to experience grateful and gracious peace. The world is a cold and cruel place sometimes. But if Jesus went through what He did just so I can have righteous salvation, then the least I can do is not look a gift horse in the mouth! I choose to survive the fireballs that Satan casts in my direction!

It is comforting to know that "peace" is mentioned three hundred and twenty-nine times in the Bible. This brings us to my very favorite Bible verses: Proverbs 3:5-6, "Trust in the Lord with all your heart, and lean not on your own understanding; in all your ways submit to him, and he will make your paths straight." These two beautiful verses serve as a cornerstone in my life. These two impressive and directive verses give me peace.

Whenever I am not doing well for whatever reason, it always comes down to reminding myself to stay steadfast in my faith. Only then can God fill me and use me to glorify Him. Only then will He reward me with peace in my life. Man cannot create genuine peace for himself. Only God can truly touch the soul, and only by His grace can we have true spiritual, mental, and emotional wholeness.

Peace through God essentially happens in three ways. It happens when we appreciate and focus on salvation. It happens when we follow and rejoice in the Word of God. It happens for those who believe that God exists and that He can accomplish supernatural things in their lives. Do you realize that God sees you as perfect? God could not care less what you look like or what your accomplishments or failures are. Your sins are forgiven. Your faults are forgotten. All God desires in return for His blessings is for you to come to Him, worship Him, and glorify Him. You accomplish this through your prayers and by living as true to His Word as possible. You do not need to impress God because He loves you just as you are! Know it, believe it, and accept God's gift of love and salvation. When you do, it will be impossible for you to be anxious, afraid, angry, or guilty. To put it simply, God is all you need to experience peace.

Peace for Others and for Self

Philippians 4:7 says, "And the peace of God, which transcends all understanding, will guard your hearts and your minds in Christ Jesus." In short, no matter how damaged or messed up you are, and no matter how damaged and messed up the world is, peace is your reward for placing your confidence in God and by having faith in Him. It is one of those times when doing less is honestly doing more. Lord, I love how You work! I love to watch You turn trash and turmoil into fabulous treasure!

God is so creative in the ways He works. He created us with the capacity to feel excruciating pain and sadness, as well as serenity and peace—all at the same time. We can experience outstanding loss and betrayal while choosing to believe it is all for the best because it is a part of God's plan. We can choose to find solace and peace in simple things instead of enabling Satan to wreak havoc in our lives by fueling us with shame, guilt, anger, and hopelessness.

I know this is easier said than done. In my past, I have experienced hopelessness to a point where suicide seemed the only way for me to experience peace. I made choices that prevented me from seeing how God was using me to work His divine intervention. I lost sight of the opportunities God had given me to grow. I belittled the joy and peace that I was awarded by God during my restoration process. I am grateful that my faith and appreciation for God's ways has enabled me to mature and evolve. Better late than never!

Those with mental health conditions face added challenges when it comes to accepting God's love and God's will and therefore have a harder time experiencing genuine peace. Many who struggle to function mentally and emotionally have never felt peace because of chemical imbalances or environmental factors. Those who did not have unconditional love and respect from their parents or their support system struggle when they are treated with unconditional love and respect from God. Those who are the victims of violence and negligence struggle because they have never known peace. When prayers seem to repeatedly go unanswered, small challenges can be blown out of proportion, and it is easy to believe God either does not care, or He does not exist.

Having patience and understanding is vital to having a healthy attitude, a healthy perspective, and peace. It is vital for us to have peace with God in order to have peace with others or with ourselves. God grants peace that transcends all understanding or human possibility when we trust Him and have faith in Him. God does not always work in obvious ways. We need to trust that He is always working in some way behind the scenes. There is no such thing as an unanswered prayer. Sometimes the answer is yes, sometimes it is no, and sometimes it is not yet—but always God answers. Sometimes God answers in more obvious ways, and sometimes His answers are more complicated and not immediately recognizable. Accepting God's direction is key to our experiencing peace in our lives. Sometimes this is not so easy, but it is totally worth the effort!

Chapter Nine

The Patience of the Holy Spirit

Be patient, then, brothers and sisters, until the Lord's coming. See how the farmer waits for the land to yield its valuable crop, patiently waiting for the autumn and spring rains. You too, be patient and stand firm, because the Lord's coming is near. (James 5:7-8)

So do not throw away your confidence; it will be richly rewarded. You need to persevere so that when you have done the will of God, you will receive what He has promised. (Heb. 10:35-36)

The Lord is not slow in keeping his promise, as some understand slowness. Instead, he is patient with you, not wanting anyone to perish, but everyone to come to repentance. (2 Peter 3:9)

Therefore let us stop passing judgment on one another. Instead, make up your mind not to put any stumbling block or obstacle in the way of a brother or sister. (Rom. 14:13)

Therefore, as God's chosen people, holy and dearly loved, clothe yourselves with compassion, kindness, humility, gentleness, and patience. Bear with each other and forgive one another if any of you has a grievance against someone. Forgive as the Lord forgave you. (Col. 3:12-13)

Here is a trustworthy saying that deserves full acceptance: Christ Jesus came into the world to save sinners—of whom I am the worst. But for that very reason I was shown mercy so that in me, the worst of sinners, Christ Jesus might display his immense patience as an example for those who would believe in him and receive eternal life. Now to the King eternal, immortal, invisible, the only God, be honor and glory for ever and ever. Amen. (1 Tim. 1:15-17)

Patience For and From God

I find it interesting to note that patience is mentioned some seventy times in the Bible. I admit that patience and self-control are my two most difficult disciplines to manage. When I am dealing with a severe bout of anxiety or depression, I have felt at times like my mind and body are about to explode unless I confront the source of my discomfort. There are times when it clearly would be in my best interest to wait for God to reveal His plans for me. Being told or made to wait can be difficult at best, and at worst it can feel life-threatening and debilitating for someone with a mental health condition.

I am sorry to say I have made many mistakes and lost out on healthy opportunities in life simply because I acted rashly and could not wait for God to reveal His plan. Instead of waiting for God to bless me with what He meant for me to receive, I went about trying to force doors open and imposing my will upon others. To those who have been adversely affected by things I have said and done (you know who you are) and are reading this now, I take responsibility for my actions, and I am sorry.

Lord, I would also like to formally and publicly accept responsibility for my lack of patience with Your plans for me. I realize that there have been many times when I should have trusted that eventually Your will would be revealed to me. I should have waited patiently. I am sorry. Please forgive me.

It is easy to see that patience is one of God's most utilized virtues. God has used patience over time to measure our dedication to Him. In the Bible, God required patience from those who served Him. As I sit in my office and gaze over at the poster of Jesus' family tree tacked to my wall, I cannot find one of God's servants who got everything they wanted at the time they asked for it. Many were made to wait for lengthy terms that you and I would consider unrealistic, unreasonable, or unhealthy. Put in the same position, we may have lost patience with God, and some of us may have lost faith in Him also.

But those who were true to God waited and were richly rewarded. Moses waited. Abraham and Sarah waited. Joseph waited. David waited. Job waited. Jesus' parents waited. The disciples waited. In fact, we are all waiting for the glorious end times. We pray for patience. We pray for guidance. We pray for strength. We pray for personal and global blessings. We pray for Jesus to return soon! We pray, and we trust, and we believe. And we wait.

Patience For and From Ourselves and Others

We all need to understand that many who struggle with mental health concerns have chemical imbalances that can make it difficult to have patience. When you struggle with panic attacks or paranoia, it is almost impossible to have patience. There are many good physicians out there who can help you manage the chemical aspects of depression and anxiety. There are medications that can help you manage anxiety and depression when it gets out of control. Then it requires a substantial amount of patience with the doctors and professionals who are working with you to enable you to reach your full potential. It is not a weakness to admit you need some help. In fact, it is a whole lot harder to admit you need help than it is to ignore a problem. If your mind and body are telling you that it is essentially impossible to physically and/or emotionally have patience, then please see a doctor.

Despite chemical imbalances, we must emotionally and physically manage to have patience so that we can live healthy lives. Even when things seem unreasonable, unrealistic, and unhealthy, we must continue to function. This is, of course, so much easier said than done. Satan has this way of wreaking havoc in our lives, creating crisis where there is none, and making it seem like things are worse than they are.

The difference in the management of depression and anxiety for someone who does not have a mental health condition versus someone who does, is essentially the component of time. For example, when a healthy individual gets their feelings hurt, they think things through and maybe consider that the perpetrator did not intend to portray themselves as they did. A healthy individual may ask for more information or even dismiss the comment altogether based on their history with the offender. On the other hand, someone who struggles to manage their anxiety and depression, may take comments and actions personally. For no good reason, they may overreact or behave in a way that negatively damages their reputation or their relationship with the offender.

In conclusion, taking the time to pray and ask God for help, guidance, patience, and peace, is the best thing you can do for yourself or for anyone else when confronted with anxiety or depression. Another good thing you can do is to look back after the precipitating event has past, evaluate your actions and reactions, and then make decisions about the need for further decisions, if any. Remember that God has a plan for you; He wants you to be a part of His plan. He wants you to pursue, persist, and act in ways that are responsible, showing that you are ready for what God is about to do in your life.

Chapter Ten

The Kindness and Goodness of the Holy Spirit

"But let him who boasts boast in this, that he understands and knows me, that I am Lord who practices steadfast love, justice, and righteousness in the earth. For in these I delight." (Jer. 9:24 ESV)

"I led them with cords of human kindness, with ties of love." (Hos. 11:4)

"Let the little children come to me, and do not hinder them, for the kingdom of heaven belongs to such as these." (Matt. 19:14)

Kindness and Goodness For and From God

Kindness and goodness are mentioned four hundred and forty times in the Bible. People struggle to comprehend these two traits. We are inclined to believe that Jesus was always kind to everyone: beggars, tax collectors, children, and the woman at the well. And yet it appears that Jesus was not always kind. He tipped the vendors' tables over in the temple. He got frustrated with his disciples. He called the Pharisees a brood of vipers. He even cursed a fruitless tree that died as a result.

Now I have realized that when Jesus walked the earth, He did so both as a man and as God. And we do not live in a perfect world. Aspects of our world are evil and disoriented at best. To engage in every fruit of the Spirit at all times as a human being is impossible because they are ultimately divine goals. The world is full of suffering. We do not get what we ask for immediately or all the time. We must trust that God is good all the time, but that does not mean that the world is not harsh occasionally. Our children are growing up with a lot of emphasis on games, and there are winners and losers in any competition. To choose to purchase things from a certain store or website means that another store is not getting our business. They have lost that sale. Those who lose are also part of a bigger plan. I have grown and learned more from the things that did not go my way in life than from the things that have. Both winning and losing have their life lessons.

Friend, are you asking yourself why you should bother making the effort, especially if you are going to lose? We bother because that is what God would have us do. We reap rewards when we follow God's Word. The blessings come when we live our lives the way He would have us live. When we are kind and good to others we are generously rewarded with a healthy attitude and positive self-esteem. God asks us to trust Him, to love our enemies, and to turn the other cheek. He asks us to let Him be the judge. God asks us to do these things because they are the right thing to do. The reward is a positive self-esteem and pride in knowing that we did our best to handle a difficult situation. God understands that sometimes it still hurts. He does not ask us to forget. He simply asks us to do our best. He created us after all. God put that tree in the middle of Eden knowing Adam and Eve would be tempted by its fruit. And He created us with the ability to be kind even in the most cruel and difficult situations. And so we do our best. We are rewarded on earth as well as in heaven for our efforts.

Kindness and Goodness for Ourselves and For Others

When I consider kindness for others and for myself, there are three concepts that come to mind. The first one is easy because there is generally immediate positive feedback. It is almost natural to be kind to strangers. My husband and I own two small Christian stores, and we wish all our customers a blessed day. When I go through the drive-through at McDonalds every morning and get my large sugar-free vanilla iced coffee, I wish a blessed day to those who take my order. I text my children and friends regularly just to wish them a blessed day. If I change my mind about a purchase at the grocery store, I put it back on the shelf where I found it. I try to smile and say hello to those I meet, whether I know them or not. My aim is to say these simple words whether I am having a good day or not. I wish I could say I do this solely because it is the right thing to do, but I can't. I also do it because it is self-rewarding, and it makes me feel good.

The second concept is a little harder because it is more intimate. I try to be kind to myself and considerate of my situation. I do this because it is what God wants me to do, and because it makes me feel good most of the time. This one is harder because there is a fine line between healthy self-care and selfishness. When I turn down a request from someone, I feel guilty and wish I could do more. But God created me to be capable of just so much, and therefore it must be His plan for me to set healthy limits. And I can be hard on myself when I make mistakes. I know I am not perfect, but that does not make messing up easier. When I do, I come to terms with my actions, and I move on. I do my best, and it is not always easy. I remind myself that God does include learning curves in my life for a reason. God's intentions are for me to learn from my mistakes, not to torture myself with them.

Finally, the third and final concept is harder than the first two. Remember that kindness is what God wants you to exemplify and that it requires discipline. Forgiving both yourself and others is an important aspect of kindness. Both are required by God of his children, and both can be rewarding. I have found that forgiveness of self and others requires a lot of discipline. God reveals more to us about ourselves through discipline and learned skills as we proceed through the developmental stages of life. Sometimes the damage you do to yourself or the damage someone else has done to you is so great that you need to forgive repeatedly. Regardless, forgiveness is always a kind and good thing that is necessary for fully healing.

Those with mental health conditions may struggle with kindness and goodness for various reasons. It is harder to be kind to someone when you are not in a good state of mind, although we often practice keeping our negative emotions hidden. Many with mental health conditions have environmental factors or genetic sources that make it difficult to be kind and good. In these situations, be encouraged that it is impossible not to experience kindness or goodness with God's guidance and help. It simply takes repeated efforts; sometimes the reward may not seem as great or last as long but the eternal blessings are present regardless. Starting out small with simple compliments and encouraging words for self and others can readily develop into habits of kindness and goodness. For example, some time ago I asked myself why I did not feel comfortable wishing someone a blessed day unless it was in my store. The first couple of times I was not in my store and wished someone a blessed day felt strange. Now I easily wish almost everyone I meet a blessed day. Some strangers look at me in surprise, and those that know me have come to return my good wishes. Regardless, it is a rewarding activity that helps me feel good about myself and about my faith. I hope you will try it and I pray it will help you too!

Chapter Eleven

The Faithfulness of the Holy Spirit

Now faith is the substance of things hoped for, the evidence of things not seen. (Heb. 11:1 NKJV)

If any of you lacks wisdom, you should ask God, who gives generously to all without finding fault, and it will be given to you. But when you ask, you must believe and not doubt, because the one who doubts is like a wave of the sea, blown and tossed by the wind. (James 1:5-6)

For by grace you have been saved through faith, and that is not of yourselves; it is the gift of God." (Eph. 2:8 NKJV)

For we walk by faith, not by sight. (2 Cor. 5:7 NKJV)

The Lord is faithful to all his words and kind in all his works. (Ps. 145:13)

> And without faith it is impossible to please God
> because anyone who comes to him must believe
> that he exists and that he rewards those who
> earnestly seek him. (Heb. 11:6)

Faithfulness For and From God

Faithfulness might only be mentioned thirty-six or so times in
the Bible, but for me, this fruit of the Spirit is one of the easiest
to comprehend. However, sometimes it is the most difficult to do.
If I put it bluntly, either you have faith, or you don't. Either you
believe that Jesus came to earth and died for your sins so that you
might receive salvation, or you don't. Either you believe that God
exists, and that He is present every day and in every way, or you
don't. Either you believe God's plans for you are for good, and that
when you follow God's Word and guidance His light will shine
upon you, or you don't. Believing only in certain circumstances
is not an option. Doubt is not an option. When you have faith in
God, He has faith in you. That's all, that's it.

Only it is not. It is too bad our relationships with God are not
black and white. For someone with mental health symptoms it can
be easy to be angry with God regarding personal circumstances or
because of a mental health condition. It can be easy to blame God
and question why He does not fix problem issues. And having
faith in a God who does not seem to be readily available and
physically present can pose a problem. Finally, those who suffer
from mental health conditions tend to have emotions that run
fast and strong. As with the fruits of kindness and goodness, with

faithfulness it is necessary to take time to stop and reason with negative emotions so the thoughts and behaviors which follow are reasonable, realistic, and healthy.

I believe that God calls us to serve Him in two ways. First, we are to please God. When we listen to the Holy Spirit and read God's Word, He promises to reward us both on earth and in heaven. When we focus our lives on the fruit of the Spirit, God has promised to reward us on earth as He will in heaven. This is significant because we have a choice to live as healthy Christians regardless of what the world throws at us. God is not the creator of the evils of this world. We must succeed despite Satan's temptations and chaos.

Our second calling is to share the good news that Jesus died for our sins so that we may live in heaven. God promises to reward us in heaven and on earth. Whenever I am privileged with an opportunity to disciple others, I feel mentally and physically rewarded. When I read and learn about those who have sacrificed their lives for Christ, the one common factor each seems to have is a sense of pride and self-confidence. These are positive and rewarding emotions. It also helps to remember that God promises to judge those who persecute others.

Long ago when I was working on my master's degree in college, I was assigned to write a personal "mission statement" by which I would live each day. My mission statement is: "To worship, praise, thank, and glorify God to the best of my ability every day in every way." I have made it my purpose in life to listen to God when He speaks to me. I have done my best to follow His will for me. I have done my best to believe that God has my back and my best interests in mind and heart. I choose to trust that in His time God will meet my needs and make known His will for me. This is not always easy. I have made many mistakes and have come to many wrong conclusions about what I thought God had in mind for me. Still in the end, when I look back on how God has influenced my direction in life, it has all been worth it. In return for my faithfulness in God, He has had faith in me; as a result He has blessed me in ways I could never have imagined!

Faith in Ourselves and In Others

One thing is certain: those with mental health conditions—and many who do not have them—still have issues with self-confidence and self-esteem. We tend to exaggerate our circumstances and symptoms. We tend to overreact and make mistakes when judging others or circumstances. We hold grudges and take things or ourselves too seriously. These behaviors lead to fear, guilt, and shame. These emotions contribute to additional complications and consequences, and more fear and guilt and shame. This never-ending cycle leads to hopelessness and despair, or even to suicidal tendencies.

I have found repeatedly that the only way to win this game is not to play. Taking a deep breath and slowing things down by reasoning with yourself and evaluating what is really going on can be very productive. Closing your eyes and asking God to lift the burden from your shoulders can be very powerful. You may need to do this repeatedly, especially if Satan rears his ugly head and you doubt that God will interfere on your behalf.

By the way, it is okay to get mad at God. He has big shoulders. He can handle it if you scream at Him occasionally and let Him know that you are sick and tired of being sick and tired. God gets it. I cannot imagine what it must be like for Him to look upon His world and see what a mess we have made of things. God sticks around because He loves us so much—much more than words can describe. God loves us as His children in the same way (but infinitely more) that we love our own children. He does not abandon us just because we throw temper tantrums occasionally. God also appreciates it when we take responsibility for our ranting afterwards; and He is quick to forgive when we ask. If letting go so we can let God have control means expressing frustration occasionally, then go for it! Just remember that giving God control truly means letting go and not holding on to grudges against people. That resistance will damage your personal relationship with God in the long run. This also includes letting go of grudges against God, which can be much easier said than done.

Chapter Twelve

The Gentleness of the Holy Spirit

You have given me the shield of your salvation. Your gentleness has made me great. (2 Sam. 22:36 ESV)

Let your gentleness be known to all men. The Lord is at hand. (Phil. 4:5 NKJV)

Gentle words cause life and health. (Prov. 15:4 TLB)

A gentle answer turns away wrath, but a harsh word stirs up anger. (Prov. 15:1)

Gentleness For and From God

For me, gentleness is one of the easier fruits of the Spirit to adhere to. It is mentioned in the Bible over fifty times. Jesus was a definite role model of this attribute. He was kind to everyone: the sick and diseased, those who put Him down, the unbelievers, the tax-collectors, and even those who persecuted Him. Jesus chewed Peter out when he cut off the ear of a soldier during Jesus' arrest as He was betrayed by Judas. Gentleness seems to rain down on us from God every minute of every day in some form or another. It is evident when you consider that no matter how bad things seem to be, they can always be worse. Gentleness is evident from God as He answers all our prayers, regardless of what the answer is. Therefore, I find it a blessing when I succeed in praising God and honoring Him with my prayers and through music.

I admit that sometimes my actions and words and even my prayers are not always gentle. There are times when I get frustrated with myself and others. There are times when the answers to my prayers are frustrating for me because they are not what I want them to be, or they are not within my desired timing. I believe that God sees me as being gentle toward Him when He hears my prayers, regardless of their content. Don't you feel that someone is doing you a favor whenever they choose to talk to you about something that is bothering them? Don't you feel better when someone talks to you about something you said or did, rather than have them complain to someone else? I believe God feels the same way. He loves us regardless of our thoughts and feelings for Him.

Gentleness for Ourselves and Others

It may not always seem that we deserve to be treated with gentleness, or that others deserve this. Our world and the people in it seem to be moving towards being more and more cruel and harsh. It seems that the morals and values of our people and our nation are becoming more and more selfish and less sacred.

The Golden Rule, which comes from Mathew 7:12 states, "Do unto others as you would have them to unto you." This to me is the cornerstone of gentleness for self and others. I find it interesting that we often treat others better than we treat ourselves. Those with mental health issues may especially find this challenging. We feel guilty and irresponsible when we treat others badly. With my mental health challenges, sometimes this even happens during the process of the interaction. I see myself and hear myself interact in ways that I know are unhealthy, yet I cannot seem to help myself. Then I feel guilty and terrible afterwards.

God understands and appreciates that we not perfect. God gets that Satan's methods are powerful when we allow him to influence our actions and interactions. Placing the blame where it belongs can help you find peace. Although I understand that I cannot justify my actions or interactions by dumping on Satan, I also understand that Satan's actions deserve my blame. It is important to appreciate that you are the only one who can do anything about your behavior. You should take your resentment to God, do your best not to repeat mistakes, and take responsibility for your actions to the best of your ability. Finally, there are times when you should simply give yourself a break. You cannot change the past, but you can control what effect your past has on your future endeavors. This is the way it works simply because God created us to work this way, and for that I am grateful. What a relief!

Chapter Thirteen

The Self-Control of the Holy Spirit

Like a city whose walls are broken through is a man who lacks self-control. (Prov. 25:28)

The one who has knowledge uses words with restraint, and whoever has understanding is even-tempered. Even fools are thought wise if they keep silent, and discerning if they hold their tongues. (Prov. 17:27-28)

His divine power has given us everything we need for a godly life through our knowledge of him who called us by his own glory and goodness. Through these he has given us his very great and precious promises, so that through them you may participate in the divine nature, having escaped the corruption in the world caused by evil desires. For this very reason, make every effort to add to your faith goodness; and to goodness, knowledge;

and to knowledge, self-control; and to self-control, perseverance; and to perseverance, godliness; and to godliness, mutual affection; and to mutual affection, love. For if you possess these qualities in increasing measure, they will keep you from being ineffective and unproductive in your knowledge of our Lord Jesus Christ. But whoever does not have them is nearsighted and blind, forgetting that they have been cleansed from their past sins. (2 Peter 1:3-9)

Self-control For and From God

For most of this book we have talked about leaning on God and going to Him with our struggles is the most beneficial thing we can do. We know as Christians in our heads, in our hearts, and in our souls that God is all-powerful, always good, and always there.

Still, we live in a busy world that is heavily influenced by Satan. The sly devil initiates chaos at every turn and propels us through evil temptations every minute of every day. It becomes easy to forget about giving God control of our thoughts and emotions. Sometimes we get going so fast we do not realize we are in an out-of-control, downward spiral until it is too late. For those with mental health conditions, add on a history of mistakes and failures, poor genetic dispositions, chronic chemical imbalances, and the struggle for self-control that is needed to obey and follow God, and maintaining self-control seems ridiculously complicated and intensely overwhelming.

Even though it may not seem like it at times, God generally rewards us with a most precious gift—the gift of time. Because of my mental health condition, I do not always feel like I can take time to breathe or to calm down, but I do my best. When I take time in the mornings and throughout each day for prayer and meditation, it makes my whole day go better! When I take time to thank and praise God for all He does for me regularly, and I constantly show my appreciation for the small things in my life, I feel better! I am less anxious about small things, and I have more self-control when temptation comes my way. When I take time to give God the glory for those things I know would never have come true without Him, it lightens my heart and soul; my thoughts become clearer. When I take time for prayer and meditation, my emotions are calmer, and my heart is more peaceful. I find it easier to engage in love, joy, peace, patience, kindness, goodness, faithfulness, gentleness, and yes, even self-control.

God is always present and can do anything, but we need to take time to remember to ask Him into our lives. We need His presence to be felt and for Him to work His wonders. Far be it for us to have self-control on our own. Fortunately, we are not alone. When we ask God for His help and trust Him to take control, problems with self-control vanish and we find peace. Friend, asking God to take control and remove your burdens requires a conscious effort. Fortunately God is always present in all ways, all the time! I pray you will take the time to ask God to manage the burdens you are facing. The sense of peace you will have as a result will be entirely worth your time!

Self-Control For and From Ourselves

While self-control is mentioned about 174 times in the Bible, perhaps you would agree that self-control is one of the most difficult characteristics to manage. Knowing what God would want us to do and living the life God would have us live despite present influences and expectations, is not easy. Unhealthy behaviors are modeled in society in so many ways today. Some of these influences are obvious, such as the violence and sex on television and other social media sources. Some influences are not so obvious, such as those included in advertisements or on the news. Regardless, ideas from negative information received from evil sources can lead to temptations to think, believe, feel, and act in ways that sadly do not measure up to God's standards. And, as mentioned previously, it is even harder for those who struggle with mental health conditions to slow down their thought processes long enough to contrive healthy alternatives to unhealthy impulses.

Most of us make conscious efforts to be good Christians. We even make resolutions every New Year's holiday in an effort to have more self-control over unhealthy habits. Sadly, we get busy with life and often fall back into unhealthy and unchristian habits. Satan is sneaky; he eases his way back into our lives, tempting us to justify those unhealthy behaviors, and encouraging us to return to the errors of our ways.

When it comes to self-control over unreasonable, unrealistic, and unhealthy thoughts, feelings, and behaviors, one of the greatest gifts God gives us is that of time. Satan acts as though it is one of his finest accomplishments to make many problems seem life-threatening. But there really is time to stop, pray, meditate, and think things through most of the time. Even a moment or two of asking God for help and guidance can give the Holy Spirit time to intercede on your behalf.

Friend, believe me! I understand how difficult this is for those of us who struggle with mental health conditions. You are not perfect. You will make mistakes, some of them repeatedly. You will get frustrated with yourself and with others for not always or effectively withstanding Satan's maneuvers. Information is power. Hang in there! One of the best things you can do is to learn from your mistakes and through prayer, meditation, counseling, and journaling. Reach out to God and to others who will support you interpersonally and casually. Don't give Satan the satisfaction of watching you slide. Develop a picture in your mind of what happens to him when you make baby steps forward. I like to picture Satan melting away like The Wicked Witch of the West in *The Wizard of Oz* whenever I choose the high road after I have previously chosen a low road. Remember, it truly is up to you! God gave you the power to follow Him and He will love and treasure you regardless and always!

Chapter Fourteen

Finding Contentment

As for me, I am in your hands; do with me
whatever you think is good and right. (Jer. 26:14)

I know what it is to be in need, and I know what
it is to have plenty. I have learned the secret of
being content in any and every situation whether
well fed or hungry, whether living in plenty or in
want. (Phil 4:12)

But godliness with contentment is great gain. For
we brought nothing into the world, and we can
take nothing out of it. (1 Tim. 6:6-7)

As this book ends, I find myself struggling with one of the things
many of us find challenging—the question of whether I will be
satisfied with the outcome of my efforts. You see, in many ways
I feel like a hypocrite because I am sitting here typing all these
wonderful words that hopefully you will find inspiring when I
am still often struggling to follow my own advice. Satan still gets

to me regularly. I do not always succeed in thinking or acting on those qualities outlined in the fruit of the Spirit. It makes me sad to admit this, however I feel empowered that I have the courage to admit my weaknesses and know what I can do about them.

My final words of advice for those of you who share my struggle with a mental health condition is to do your best to be content with what you have. Desire more, but do not need more to be happy. I may sound like a broken record when I say that things could always be worse. Someone said once that where there is a will, there is a way. God gave you your will and He lights the way! I pray that you will find ways to be happy with what you have; desire more, but do not need more to be happy.

If anything, this book was written honestly. Although I have not experienced exactly what you have, I pray that some tidbit written here rings true for you or for someone you know. Although I have no idea who will read or be influenced by this book, I choose to believe it was not written in vain. Know that you are loved, and that somewhere I am praying that you are living the fruit of the Spirit! The Father, Son, and Holy Spirit love you, too, and will bless your relationship with them wherever you go!

Yours in Christ,
God Bless!

Heide Kuhlman

Reflections

Reflections

Reflections

Reflections

Reflections

Reflections

Reflections

Reflections

Reflections

Reflections

Reflections

Reflections

Reflections

Reflections

Reflections

Printed in the United States
by Baker & Taylor Publisher Services